Reflections in time

Clarence "Sonny" White

Copyright © 2011 by Clarence "Sonny" White

Reflections in time
by Clarence "Sonny" White

Printed in the United States of America

ISBN 9781619044975

All rights reserved solely by the author. The author guarantees all contents are original and do not infringe upon the legal rights of any other person or work. No part of this book may be reproduced in any form without the permission of the author. The views expressed in this book are not necessarily those of the publisher.

Unless otherwise indicated, Bible quotations are taken from King James version. Copyright © 1976 by Thomas Nelson, Inc, Nashville, Tennessee.

www.xulonpress.com

REFLECTIONS IN TIME
(the book) (index)

A Masters Touch 9

A Place Called Home 10

A Place Of Memory 12

Breath Of Life 14

Christmas (The reason for the season) 16

Country Winding Roads 18

Don't Burn A Bridge 19

Enough Said 20

Flowers In God's Garden 21

God Sees Every Tree 22

Gods Message Of Love 24

Homecoming 26

Home For Christmas 27

Jesus Is The Reason (for the season) 29

Just A Few Miles Down The Road 30

Just Half The Man 32

Lasting Impression 33

Liberty Baptist Church Christmas Bake Sale 34

Life Before God—Life After God 36

Little Eyes—Little Ears 37

Lord I Need Your Help Today (a husbands prayer) 38

My Over The Counter Medication 40

On Fathers Day (2010) 42

On Mothers Day 44

Our Little Country Church 45

Powered By Love 47

Protector 49

Put Christ Back In Christmas (this year) 51

Reflecting Back On Life 53

Reflections In Time 54

Reflections of Life 56

Reflections in time

Remember When 58

Remembering A Friend 60

Renewal 62

Safe Passage 64

Satan Came To Church Today 65

Shining Example 66

Stand As A Man 67

Start Loving Jesus First 69

Sunday Christians 71

Thank You Lord 73

The 50s Drug Problem 74

The First Christmas 76

Thoughts of a Snowman 77

Walk A Mile In Their Shoes 79

What Jesus Wouldn't Do 83

Who's Counting 85

A MASTER'S TOUCH

My cup it runneth over
Such beauty he hath made
This week I viewed a work of art
A Master had displayed

Painstakingly it was crafted
Such perfection I'm amazed
Painted from the heart a work of art
The whole world being his stage

Such an array of vivid colors
Each tree perfectly in place
A perfect picture of peace on earth
A reflection of God's grace

Each fall our Lord and Master
Reflects love more than words can say
Allowing trees change their summer dress
And puts his paintings on display

Nothing short of spectacular
Created like none other can
But painted by the Master
All part of a master plan

Nothing was spared, no price to great
He worked with nail scarred hands
Worth more than gold, his beauty to behold
For those who love the man

© October 2007 Clarence "Sonny" White

A Place Called Home

I drive down the familiar winding road
To a place I still call home
Along a broken down, wooden picket fence
That once boasted a plush green lawn

The old house has weathered many years
Yet stands proud against the sky
The porch swing hangs, by only one chain
And the well most certainly dry

The front yard once filled with the laughter
And antics of five happy kids
Now overgrown with grass and weeds
The flower garden now very well hid

Driving thru the gate, now broken down
Eyes glued to the kitchen door
My heart beats fast, I'm home at last
Like all other times before

Vision blurred, eyes damp with tears
I still see her in my mind
She runs to me; "Welcome home son,
It's been such a long, long time

But this time Mom won't be here
Like me, she too, is home
She passed the test, she's with the best
Around God's golden throne

And before I leave, as always
I kneel to God in prayer
And thank him for precious memories
And for a Mom who was always there

© May 2008 Clarence "Sonny" White

Written in honor of my Mother;
Cora Lee (Handley) White

A PLACE IN MEMORY

The chimney stood some twenty years
The old house long fallen down
Marking a spot of memories and birth
Some two or three miles north of town

Memories that linger forever
And still bring a smile to my face
Reminiscing the joy of a freckle face boy
Playing around the old home place

The muddy Hatchie River, ever so close
Where often I tossed in a line
Watching the cork drop out of sight
Hoping for a big one this time

Under surveillance of several green frogs
Lining the bank at rivers edge
Croaking complaints of intrusion
By some young, short whip-snapper kid

Mark, my best friend always by my side
We were happy, a boy and his dog
Exploring for hours deep in the woods
Then resting on an old hollow log

If trees could talk, stories they'd tell
Of all the good times that we had
A mixed shepherd/collie companion
And a pre-teen dark headed lad

When I get to Heaven, see Mom and Dad
I know everything will be fine
And please God a house with a chimney
With a muddy river running close by

© December 16, 2009 Clarence "Sonny" White

BREATH OF LIFE

Things going bad again today
Seems nothing works out right
The same persistent headache
Awake half of the night

Laid off from your job again
With bills all coming due
Landlord threatens to evict
You don't know what to do

Grass too high, mower broke
You can't afford to fix
City calls about complaints
You better cut it quick

Tension keeps on building up
About to blow a fuse
Friends I know a man who can
I really have good news

Jesus wants to bear your load
It's not really the end
He only waits for you to ask
He's ready to begin

Jesus knows our every thought
And everything we need
He's our Lord and Saviour
And he's a friend indeed

Suffocating in a sea of sin
Want something to relieve
Jesus is the breath of life
We only need to breathe

© October 2010 Clarence "Sonny" White

CHRISTMAS

(The reason for the season)

A blanket of new fallen snow
Paint the fields a glistening white
Reflected by the moon, purity
On a cold clear Christmas Eve night

Kinfolks are here visiting
To help us celebrate
This years Christmas holiday
Everything will be so great

Stockings hanging by the fireplace
Children wide eyed with awe
So excited they can't sleep
And there's talk of Santa Claus

The smell of food is prevalent
Ham and turkey being baked
Potatoes, corn and cranberry sauce
Man, I can hardly wait

Yet, something is missing
Something is not quite right
Someone was not invited
Someone's not here tonight

Pondering these thoughts in my mind
I realized the worst
We failed to invite Jesus
As we celebrate his birth

We pray to you our precious Lord
And asked to be forgiven
And never-ever let us forget
The real reason for the season

Be with us each and very day
Guide our thoughts and minds
And always Jesus, be our guest
Especially at Christmas time

© December 2005 Clarence "Sonny" White

COUNTRY WINDING ROADS

Autumn leaves, red, yellow, brown
Float like feathers to the ground
Splashing colored patterns unseen before
On Country roads I must explore

A winding road I'll travel again
Curious, what lies, beyond the bend
Over the hill and across the creek
Rewarded with the wonders I seek

Multicolored leaves, blue skies above
Reflections of our Masters love
Reminding as I continue my quest
God always gives his very best

Driving across the babbling brook
Intrigued, I have to stop and look
At hundreds of painted, floating leaves
Blown gently by an autumn breeze

Like many tiny ships with masts
In awe of God's creations I gasp
As they sail across in majestic pride
Eager to reach the other side

Disappointed, I must head home again
And leave this road that has no end
One thing I know, where ever I roam
Country winding roads always lead home

© October 2009 Clarence "Sonny" White

DON'T BURN A BRIDGE

It seems God spoke to me today
About letting pride get in the way
Too quick to judge and sometimes hate
And Heaven forbid: retaliate

Sometimes we let emotions guide
And common sense they over-ride
Words are said out of hurt and spite
Then later impossible to make things right

We've hurt ourselves beyond repair
Now hard to tell a friend we care
We suffer from self inflicted wounds
Too much said and spoken too soon

Overcome with shame we hang our head
Much too late, the words already said
Words causing pain like a heart attack
Yet, there's never a way to take them back

So let's be careful, what we say
Try not to let pride get in the way
In everything we say and do
Remember other folks have feelings too

Perhaps, leave these thoughts in our head
It's better sometimes leaving words unsaid
Better not to burn a bridge my friend
We may need to pass this way again

© February 2008 Clarence "Sonny" White

**

ENOUGH SAID

Were you in Church this morning
And did you look down your nose
At a portly, balding gentleman
His buttons tugging at his clothes

And did you say to someone
Or perhaps think on just a whim
Why he's so fat and ugly
Thank God I'm not like him

Perhaps you think you're better
Because you're dressed so neat
Have a new car and a house to live in
That keeps you off the street

Do you have no compassion
Just really do not care
You know I believe my Bible reads
We entertain Angels, unaware

I might have been that gentleman
And I give thanks to God above
The God that made you—he made me too
I too, am covered by his blood

© June 3, 2003 Clarence "Sonny" White

FLOWERS IN GODS GARDEN

The sun may not shine today
The sky may not be blue
But there's one thing for certain
God will be there for you

We are flowers in His garden
He nurtures us each day
As we strive for perfection
To be picked for his bouquet

We should blossom at our finest
To reflect his love and grace
Happy to be a child of God
For soon we'll see his face

We'll forever be with Jesus
Heavenly mansions to explore
Where we will live forever
And time will be no more

So be ever-ready when he comes
That he may pick with pride
When Jesus comes to earth again
Returning for his bride

© September 12, 2010 Clarence "Sonny" White

GOD SEES EVERY TREE

God reminds us many times
To think before we speak
Consider those it will affect
And how far it will reach

Make sure we are qualified
When we try to make the call
If we hurt a Christian neighbor
Is it really worth it all

They say," hindsight's 20/20
But we're really going blind"
An old familiar saying
We hear from time to time

We can't rescind a spoken word,
Mend a broken heart
Or put together pieces
Of a world that's torn apart

I write to you, Oh Christian friends
To remind you of God's love
And of his forgiving
When asked of him above

Pray for God to search our hearts
Give stubbornness a shove
Remove all inner bitterness
And replace it with his love

Mistakes are made quite often
By mortals such as we
For men see only forest
But God sees every tree

© May 2008 Clarence "Sonny" White

GOD'S MESSAGE OF LOVE

I feel God spoke
To me today
He mentioned you
And by the way
He wanted to
Make sure I say

He loves you

He knows the trials
You're going thru
He reminds us Jesus
Had trials too
But remember God
Can make things new

He loves you

It's satan's plan
You be confused
And from God's ark
Of safety, removed
But God gave his son
To die for you

He loves you

The stakes are high
Rewards are great
But remember satan
Lies in wait
Let God remove you
From this fate

He loves you

When times are bad
And life's not fair
Just close your eyes
And say a prayer
Believe in God
He's always there

He loves you

From this cold world
Come where it's warm
Let God protect you
From the storm
He waits for you
With open arms

He loves you

© July 17, 2008 Clarence "Sonny" White

HOME COMING

Somewhere there's a long winding path
That leads to a beautiful place
A special path not all will find
God leads us there through faith

A place prepared by God himself
Just beyond that golden shore
Where streets are lined with solid gold
And time will be no more

A land of never ending day
No setting of the sun
A land where there's no sadness
And the Master will say well done

We'll spend eternity with Jesus
Meet friends and loved ones there
And marvel at this wondrous place
With which nothing can compare

Should you arrive before me
And see friends that we once knew
Please wait for me, it won't be long
And soon I'll follow you

© March 2006 Clarence "Sonny" White

HOME FOR CHRISTMAS

Smoke curls lazily from the chimney
And in the corner of my eye
I see the outline of Grandpa's house
Against a clear blue, moonlit sky

The narrow, winding old dirt road
Has seen much better days
Deep ruts bounce the car to and fro
But alas, this is the only way

Driving thru the gate I see Grandma
She smiles, standing at the door
And in my heart, it's home at last
Almost like times before

And in the backyards of my mind
I go back to younger years
The most pleasant time of my childhood
The time that I lived here

Going to the woods with Grandpa
Finding and cutting that perfect tree
Just Grandpa and his,"little man"
Words he most always called me

Taking the tree to the living room
We would put it in a stand
Then we would start to decorate
Grandpa and his little man

The smell of cookies overwhelming
My mouth waters as I recall
Grandma would slip me one or two
When she thought that no one saw

Dinner done then off to bed
"Say your prayers", Grandma would say
Else Santa Claus won't be stopping here
With all the presents in his sleigh

Then early Christmas morning
I'd be the first one out of bed
Checking out the Christmas tree
To see if Santa left my sled

It matter not if I got nothing
There would never be despair
We had love like God intended
A love that was always there

Suddenly I come back to reality
As Grandma calls my name
I feel the joy, but with Grandpa gone
It's not really quite the same

With all my love for Grandpa
I realize I'm not alone
God loved him too and for Christmas
God wanted Grandpa home

© November 2007 Clarence "Sonny" White

Reflections in time

JESUS IS THE REASON

(for the season)

I
know
Christmas
means to me
a gift of life, I've
been set free. When
I think of how God gave
his son, remission of sin for
everyone. How humble at his
feet I fall. He knows my heart and
he's my all. An awesome Jesus nailed
to the cross, who shed his blood to save
the lost. He died there, for you and me, that
we have life, abundantly. When you celebrate
this Christmas morn, inside with family, cozy and
warm. With presents around the Christmas tree. It's
not about—you and me. It's not what you get, or what
it's worth. It's to celebrate our Savior's birth. Remember
JESUS IS THE REASON-THE REAL REASON, FOR THE
SEASON.
Praise
his
holy
name.
Give
God
the
praise
he is due.

JESUS IS LOVE	JESUS IS LOVE
LOVE IS JESUS	LOVE IS JESUS

© December 1, 2008 Clarence "Sonny" White

JUST A FEW MILES DOWN THE ROAD

The old man sat quietly
Waiting out his time
Drawing on his bank of memories
As old thoughts filled his mind

Seems it was only yesterday
With Mom and Dad he would go
To a small vine covered country Church
Just a few miles down the road

With eager anticipation
He would gladly find a space
On a bench with other children
In this very special place

With book in hand the teacher
Would read to them a spell
All kind of Bible stories
Like Jonah and the whale

David and Goliath
Jesus ascending to above
This very special lady
Taught them all about God's love

Taught them to recite "The Lord's Prayer"
They memorized it well
Taught them there is a Heaven
And also there's a hell

It was she, who helped to shape his life
The direction he should go
In Sunday school, a little country Church
Just a few miles down the road

© October 29, 2007 Clarence "Sonny" White

Proverbs 22 verse 6 KJV; Train up a child in the way he should go: and when he is old, he will not depart from it.

JUST HALF THE MAN

As time goes on and memory goes back
It seems only yesterday
I stood in Dad's old work shoes
In a little boy's game of play

Dad would laugh, hug me tight
And say, "Son, it's in God's plan",
"But, it takes a few years and a lot of work
For a boy to be a man"

It was Dad, who taught me about God,
Took me to Church each week
It was Dad who knelt with me each night
As we prayed our souls to keep

He made me proud to be his son,
Never brought the family shame
In the words of simple Country folks
"Mr. White had a very good name"

I recall his teachings thru the years
He practiced what he preached
Not what he said, but what he did
This young man's heart he reached

Time has flown, Dad passed on
To join God's Heavenly band
"Dear Lord I'm almost twice his size,
Help me be just half the man"

© June 2, 2008 Clarence "Sonny" White

Reflections in time

LASTING IMPRESSION

We were very close all those years
Inseparable most of the time
At first I took too much for granted
Thinking all of his love was just mine

He was always so kind and loving
And could make me feel so proud
It felt wonderful just to be with him
Whether alone or even in a crowd

After several years I grew wiser
It became plain for me to see
That I was not the only one
He loved others as much as me

It mattered not, he loved others
And looking back, often I smile
I'll carry these memories to my grave
I'll pass them on to my child

It was really hard to lose him
I still cry from time to time
He helped make me better and stronger
I still picture him in my mind

For each day as I grow older
I realize more and more what I had
Most folks would call him Mr. White
But five of us called him Dad

Happy Fathers day Dad

We love you

© June 15, 2002 Clarence "Sonny" White

LIBERTY BAPTIST CHURCH (CHRISTMAS BAKE SALE)

(Humor)

It was mid-December
Christmas at the door
Colder than all blazes
I remember that for sure

A before Christmas bake sale
At Liberty Baptist Church
Christmas cakes and pies galore
You didn't have to search

The smell was overwhelming
My mouth waters as I recall
Cakes, pies and cookies
On tables along the wall

A prize was to be awarded
For one judged to be the best
A very hard decision
The Judge put to the test

Now, Sister Bertha Johnson
The Judge was her best friend
Whispered, "Try that apple pie
The second from the end"

Judge Buford was grinning
And he slightly winked an eye
As he awarded a blue ribbon
For Bertha's apple pie

About that time our hound dog
Charged thru an open door
His chain catching a table
Spilling cakes onto the floor

Folks stared in disbelief
Not knowing what to do
Watching our old hound dog
Wolf down a cake or two

Poppa wasn't very happy
That Momma didn't win
Cause she had been a winner
Time and time again

Bertha shouting oohs and aahs
Making matters worse
Poppa cut her down a notch
With one short, snappy verse

Don't act so prissy, missy
Will you for goodness sake
You may have took blue ribbon
But our hound dog took the cake

© October 2008 Clarence "Sonny" White

LIFE BEFORE GOD / LIFE AFTER GOD

Life before God	Life After God
Another day	Another year
Same place	Gone by
Life one	I smile
Rat race	Don't cry
Work hard	Don't complain
Every day	About naught
Hard work	I realize
Low pay	My fault
Truck broke	Load heavy
Can't fix	Fearsome task
Make two hundred	God help
Owe six	Just ask
Money gone	Got God
I cry	Life rhyme
Can't afford	He was there
To die	All the time
Wolf always	
At door	
Unhappy	
For sure	

© January 2008 Clarence "Sonny" White

LITTLE EYES—LITTLE EARS

God allows us to be an example
To the children he loves so dear
But it seems we may be falling short
And this is something that I fear

We shouldn't take this honor lightly
It's most certainly isn't wise
To betray the trust—God has in us
Concerning little ears and little eyes

Have you taken time to watch a child
Why, you can almost see wheels turn
They watch everything us grown ups do
To see what they can learn

Their minds are constantly recording
Everything that's in their sight
And everything they hear us say
Because grown ups must be right

So be careful of the things you say and do
And of consequences it may bring
Because little eyes are watching
And little ears hear everything

© Clarence "Sonny" White 09-03- 2003

LORD I NEED YOUR HELP TODAY
(A husband's prayer)

Lord I need your help today

I call on you in prayer

Assured like all the other times

I've called and you were there

It's nothing for myself I ask

Yet, it's such a part of me

The half you joined to me years ago

When I was young and free

The other half that made us one

That I care about so much

I pray to you on bended knees

Give her your healing touch

Reflections in time

Let her feel your tender mercy

Given in your special way

Lord, heal my wife from head to toe

I need your help today

© January 23, 2008 Clarence "Sonny" White

MY OVER THE COUNTER MEDICATION
(Song lyrics)

For a long, long time I was troubled
Grief kept pouring in
No one to turn to or talk to
Still living my life of sin

That's when Jesus found me
And turned my life around
He put joy, in this old boy
And put my feet on higher ground

He's my over the counter medication
And I need him every day
Jesus saw the need and he indeed
Made this pain in my heart go away

He said lo, I am with you always
He's in my heart to stay
He's my over the counter medication
I like it that way

Now folks if you don't know him
I'll introduce you to my friend
Ask Jesus to forgive you
Open your heart and let him in

And when you're on the road to Heaven
Climbing higher every day
Shouting and singing God's praises
I know I'll hear you say

He's my over the counter medication
And I need him every day
Jesus saw the need and he indeed
Made this pain in my heart go away

He said lo, I am with you always
He's in my heart to stay
He's my over the counter medication
I like it that way

© **November 2007 Clarence "Sonny" White**

ON FATHERS DAY (2010)

He awoke Sunday quite depressed
Reminded of what lie ahead
Not looking forward to going anywhere
He had rather sleep late instead

Sunday was always his favorite day
After working hard all week
Sleep late then watch the ball game
Get some real R & R and peace

Oh, he wanted to visit, but then again
Ball games would be on all day
What a bummer to miss any or all
Why, his favorite team would play

Guilt overrides, he knows he must go
His mind starts devising a plan
Make an appearance an hour or so
Then leave as soon as he can

He arrives at 1 pm on the nose
There's a frail man waiting outside
The old man smiles as he sees him
With so much Fatherly pride

Sorry I'm late Dad, so much to do
I can't stay as long as I planned
As Dad hugs him tight for a long time
He sees hurt in the eyes of the man

Time flew by as they reminisced
Of all the good times they had
All of a sudden it's time to go
And he says his goodbye to Dad

At a nursing home just a mile from town
An aging Father wipes away a tear
And softly whispers, "I love you Son",
"I'll see you again next year"

© May 25, 2010 Clarence "Sonny" White

Please visit Dad on Fathers day. Give him a hug and tell him how much you love him. If it's too far and impossible to go, call and tell him. Even if things have not always been the best, Jesus forgives and makes all things new. God Bless, Sonny

ON MOTHERS DAY

Too much time spent looking at cards
Meaningful gifts and such
When often we tend to overlook
What Mothers want and need so much

Don't let her wait at the nursing home
Like some of the others do
Who simply failed to show up again
You know she thinks the world of you

Oh! what she'd give for quality time
To converse with her own child
Re-living some of the good times
And bring back her beautiful smile

This Sunday forget about the lake
Or the round of golf with the boys
Spend a few hours with Mom today
It's something you'll both enjoy

Re-live with her when you were young
And some of the things you did
And maybe somewhere, down the road
You can share it with your kid

Why not give Mom the ultimate gift
It's the easiest thing to do
Don't send her flowers; "Take them"
She needs some time with you!

© May 9, 2010 Clarence "Sonny" White

Our Little Country Church

It stood there some fifty years
A beacon on the hill
A place of Godly refuge
For whosoever will

A little Church where everyone
Is welcomed at the door
A place that makes you feel at home
Like you'd been there before

No large or fancy building
To put on or impress
A simple place to seek the Lord
And put your soul at rest

We still sing the same old songs
Your Dad and Mother did
The ones you heard years ago
When you were just a kid

The people here are genuine
Guaranteed you won't be bored
Each person has the same goal
They came to seek the Lord

At times there may be only few
To seek the Lord in prayer
But numbers never mattered
The Lord is always there

The word of God is taught here
With nothing watered down
An opportunity for those who will
To turn their life around

Why not visit us this Sunday
Bible preaching and much more
Join us in Godly worship
We'll meet you at the door

© May 22, 2008 Clarence "Sonny" White

POWERED BY LOVE

A foxhole in some foreign land
Is not the place to be
But, there's a job that must be done
To keep our Country free

A life of freedom twenty years
And knowing it's a fact
It's no surprise, when needs arise
He's obliged to pay it back

Each day he strives to do his best
And make his Country proud
Living a life of pride and guts
Un-shadowed by a cloud

Bombs still bursting all around
He fights a gallant fight
No time for fear, the fight is here
And continues through the night

Thoughts go to his wife at home
And he prays a silent prayer
God protect her though the night
And cement the love that's there

Then thinking of his only son
His first Christmas tonight
Should I not return, Lord help him learn,
To choose the path that's right

"Mail call, Private White, first class"
Letters from home bring a smile
A Christmas card placed over his heart
That makes it all worth while

© November 22, 2008 Clarence "Sonny" White

Pray for our military folks. They are the BEST

PROTECTOR

Somewhere in a distant land
A young man tries to sleep
He's scared and it's dangerous
So he prays his soul to keep

He lost his buddy just last night
In a suicide bomb attack
And wonders if he'll make the night
No one to watch his back

He wonders about folks back home
Who come and go as they please
With not much to worry about
They move around with ease

About misfits that burn our flag
And march to any cause
Whose freedom he's also fighting for
This makes him stop and pause

The ones who have never worked
And have nothing to lose
Never contributed to their country
And have never paid their dues

The Soldier bounces back to reality
And he thanks dear God above
For safely keeping him though the night
And surrounding him with his love

And today he'll fight for us again
And for the old Red, White and Blue
As for the rebels without a cause
Why, he'll be fighting for them too

© **December 2004 Clarence " Sonny" White**

PUT CHRIST BACK IN CHRISTMAS THIS YEAR

(song lyrics)

Seems we've forgotten the true meaning of Christmas
In all the hurry of buying presents and things
A lot of people have started calling it Xmas
And somehow it don't have that old familiar ring

Have we forgotten it's the birthday of our Savior
And every Christmas he looks down and sheds a tear
Remember he died on the cross to save you and me, the Lost
Let's put Christ back in Christmas this year

(chorus)
Let's put Christ back in Christmas this year
Think of the true meaning each day as Christmas draws near
Stay with the basics day by day, in that old familiar way
Let's put Christ back in Christmas this year

(Talk verse) Lord, have we forgotten that night in a manger
The three wise men that followed a star
The birth of Jesus our Saviour
Lord forgive us – how foolish we are

I pray and ask for your forgiveness, Jesus
I'll write a song to help spread the message clear
We'll set aside our greed and hate, before it's too late
And put Christ back in Christmas this year

(chorus)
Let's put Christ back in Christmas this year
Think of the true meaning each day as Christmas draws near
Stay with the basics day by day, in that old familiar way
Let's put Christ back in Christmas this year

© 1982 Clarence "Sonny" White
© 2007 Clarence "Sonny" White

REFLECTING BACK ON LIFE

I stood at the crossroads
Not knowing which way
To turn, the left or the right
Reflecting back thru the years
Thru heartaches and tears
And the mess I made of my life

Now I didn't steal
And I didn't kill
And I never intended to hurt
Any family or friend
But did again and again
As I scooped up and ran with the dirt

It's surprising I lived
But Jesus forgives
And forgave a poor wretch like me
I acknowledged my sin
Asked him to come in
To my heart and he set me free

Now I'll sing his praise
For the rest of my days
But my friend, how about you
Ask forgiveness and love
Feel it flow from above
Sing his praise as you start life anew

© January 28, 2009 Clarence "Sonny" White

REFLECTIONS IN TIME

Did you ever dream
Of going back in time
Leaving your cares
And worries behind

To an innocent age
A time of youth
When God had our trust
And we spoke the truth

When parents led us
In bedtime prayer
Real happy times
When love was there

We obeyed grandparents
Mom and Dad
And who can forget
The good times we had

When heroes won
The real good guys
Not now the case
My, how time flies

Bobby socks
And blue suede shoes
Dads old Chevy
A Sunday cruise

A swimming hole
On a sunny day
In a high barn loft
Covered with hay

Problems were small
And folks were kind
Etched in memory
Reflections in time

© August 11, 2008 Clarence "Sonny" White

REFLECTIONS OF LIFE

Beautiful flowers by the pulpit
In a magnificent array
Bring back to me, old memories
Of another time, of bygone days

It was here I first heard the word
Preached so many different ways
The once new varnished pulpit
Now like me, weathered and aged

It was here that I first believed
And here I accepted the Lord
It was at this altar by the pulpit
Where we prayed in one accord

It was here I was baptized
According to God's will
Immersed, came up a brand new man
Making God so much more real

It was here we were joined together
To start a brand new life
No longer just man and woman
But now a husband and a wife

It was here I brought my children
So they might learn of Jesus' ways
And here they received their teaching
So they may never stray

Reflections in time

And it's here I'll be one last time
As I go to meet the man
My funeral preached from this pulpit
The same place it all began

© November 2007 Clarence "Sonny" White

REMEMBER WHEN

Remember when we put God first
And lived by the golden rule
Before Post Office and School shootings
When God was still in School

When Teachers were allowed to teach
And to discipline as well
When Ministers preached Gods word
To save our souls from hell

When everyone respected the law
Policemen were in charge
Lack of money didn't determine guilt
And criminals didn't run at large

Growing up and getting a job
Was every young mans dream
Back when sex was dirty
And the air we breathed was clean

The word "terrorist" caused no fear
We thought of overseas
Maybe in some place far away
Not close to you and me

If God allowed you to live this long
He has a plan for you
Friend, it's time you straighten up
Do what God would have you do

There's no guarantee of tomorrow
Unless you accept Jesus Christ as Lord
If you're about to miss the boat
You better get on board

Ask Jesus to forgive your sins
Live by the golden rule
Obey all of Gods commandments
And put God back in our Schools

© January 1, 2002 Clarence "Sonny" White

REMEMBERING A FRIEND

The cruel words stung hard
In the back of my brain
Dry lips searched for words
But the words never came

Shock waves and tingling
Running all thru my head
Results not what I hoped for
The Doctor had said

The tests were positive
But how can this be
It happens to others
But certainly not me

That awful word "Cancer"
Still echoes thru my mind
The word that strikes terror
At almost any time

The drive back to home
Seemed ten times as long
No joy in my heart
No singing happy songs

I stumble thru my door
As the tears start to flow
Swollen rivers of tears
From deep in my soul

I dropped to my knees
Thinking this was the end
But then I remembered
My Lord, Saviour and friend

Now the cancer is gone
And I'm good as new
All praise and glory to God
To whom all praise is due

© August 24, 2007 Clarence "Sonny" White

"What a friend we have in Jesus————"

RENEWAL

Morning sun, barely in sight
Sparkling diamonds reflect the light
Sunshine warms the morning dew
Shades of green beneath skies of blue

Half way up, the old Oak tree
From their nest, protected, free
Baby robins, mouths open wide
As mother drops the food inside

Baby rabbits scamper around
Carefree, playing, on the ground
Fruit trees blossom, a wide array
Of beautiful colors, God has made

The winding creek, water so clear
Fish are seen and you can hear
Brrump, brrump of large green frogs
At water's edge on fallen logs

A red fox plays in meadows green
Occasionally a baby fox is seen
I stand in awe, joy has no end
As God shares, with me his friends

Reminding, with spring comes renew
Not unlike life, God made for you
Accepting God, new life begins
Under the blood goes all our sin

Reflections in time

God gave his son for you and me
That we have life, abundantly
Our life will never be the same
Give him thanks and praise his name.

© March 21, 2009 Clarence "Sonny" White

SAFE PASSAGE

God reminds us life is a wisp
Like a vapor it's here and gone
All that's left are memories
We leave that linger on

Tho we may be Heaven bound
I think most would agree
Memories of love and pleasant thoughts
Are what we desire to leave

God said rejoice at the passing
Of a loved one heaven bound
To spend eternity with Jesus
Who God's love will surround

At the passing of a loved one
We too die a little inside
But death is a bridge all must cross
To get to the other side

© *July 2007 Clarence "Sonny" White*

SATAN CAME TO CHURCH TODAY

Satan came to Church today
Did evil work, then went away
Yet, something he doesn't understand
You destroy the body but not the man

Satan's work is evil and grim
Death and destruction follow him
Should this be the path you choose
Hell awaits, your life you lose

To Satan, we will never bow
We emerge even stronger now
The body destroyed God takes us home'
To be with him around his throne

God has prepared for us place
We'll worship him and see his face
In Heaven where new life begins
Forevermore, time has no end

For those who serve God, my friend
Life's not over, it just begins
The physical body dead and gone
The soul lives on, and on and on

© March 2009 Clarence "Sonny" White

**IN MEMORY OF PASTOR FRED WINTERS PASTOR OF MARYVILLE, ILLINOIS FIRST BAPTIST CHURCH

SHINING EXAMPLE

Last Sunday I watched a brother
Walk into the house of God
Along an old familiar path
His feet had often trod

His walk is somewhat slower now
But his goal remains the same
To attend God's house of worship
And praise his holy name

Although he uses a walker
To help steady his walk
I've never heard the man complain
When I've listened to him talk

I prayed to God to be like him
And have no complaints at all
The biggest man I've ever seen
Slightly over five feet tall

We've learned by his examples
Watching what he would do
And remember in your daily walk
People will be watching you

He let his light shine over ninety years
I think we should applaud
An inspiration and a blessing
God bless you, "Brother Claude"

© June 4, 2006 Clarence "Sonny" White

In memory of brother Claude Harris

STAND AS A MAN

I heard the word preached many times before
But tonight would not be the night
Oh, I intended to give my heart to God
But in a week or so would be alright

What would friends think of me on my knees
And of a young man that actually prays
I'm young, there's more time and I can wait
But, I'll do it one of these days

Days turned to weeks, weeks turned to months
And still I continued to wait
Not realizing the danger of putting it off
Not dreaming, I procrastinate

Forgetting God could come any day
At a time that no one can tell
Always dreaming of going to Heaven
Never wanting to wind up in Hell

Out of the blue, a sharp stinging pain
Deep in the left side of my chest
Suddenly I realize, I'm not right with God
Oh God, I'm not ready I confess

Waking up I hear voices, tho I cannot see
I still hear the words that they say
In horror I realize they're talking about me
Saying he probably won't make it today

Tears well in my eyes as I try to pray
And continue to roll down my face
Remembering the words of the Pastor last week
"Come boldly to the throne of grace"

Him preaching not to be ashamed of Jesus
Not in anything that we do
Reminding if we are ashamed of Jesus
Then he will be ashamed of us too

As I pray to God nothing else matters
He gave me strength to help me take a stand
God has given me the courage to face anything
And the courage to stand as a man

Boldly and unashamed, I call out his name
Asking forgiveness and he answers my call
All praise and glory to a forgiving, healing God
Whose grace is sufficient for all

II Corinthians 12 verse 9 KJV: My grace is sufficient for thee; for my strength is made perfect in weakness.

© September 1, 2007 Clarence "Sonny" White

START LOVING JESUS FIRST

Last Wednesday night in service
A brother stood and spoke
The words of John—inspired by God
Of things worthy to note

In the book of Revelations
Our Father up above
Said," I have somewhat against thee
Because thou hast left thy first love"

As a brother has explained
Revelation two and fourth verse
God has somewhat against us
Because we stopped loving Jesus first

And reading in the Bible
You will find many a verse
Reminding us God is a jealous God
And wants us to put him first

He's the alpha and omega
The beginning and the end
Thou shalt have no other God before him
That means you and me, my friend

If you would search the commandments
The first and greatest you would find
"Thou shalt love the Lord thou God
With all thy heart, thy soul and thy mind"

The second; love thy neighbor as thyself
Which is like unto the first
On these two commandments hang the law
Matthew 22, fortieth verse

Jesus Christ is the living water
For all of those who thirst
Give him the praise and glory
Start loving Jesus first

© Clarence "Sonny" White September 2002

SUNDAY CHRISTIANS

(What not to be)

Another Monday morning
A lot of traffic on the road
Angrily, I said a few bad words
To a selfish road hogging toad

Shouting attracts the local police
Driving like I'm going to a fire
With my "Jesus" bumper sticker on
They thought I had stole the car

I finally slip in to work
An hour late again
The boss man didn't know it
So I'll have him sign me in

And my nosy secretary
I call her nosy Rose
I let her know, she rats on me
And out the door she goes

I make it to Friday evening
Without collapsing on the floor
Stop for one at the watering hole
But then have several more

Saturday morning at the local pub
Playing cards and telling jokes
Missed men's prayer breakfast again
Cussed out some drunken bloke

I get up Sunday morning
After another week in sin
Dust off the family Bible
And I'm off to Church again

But I'm a decent person folks
I don't really do any wrong
Cause I go to Church on Sunday
And I sing Christian songs

© Clarence "Sonny" White February 2008

THANK YOU LORD

Today I stand before you Lord
And I stand in awe of you
I give you praise and thank you Lord
For all the things you do

You're always there when I'm in need
Ready to answer prayer
I have only to ask and believe, dear Lord
Anyday, anytime, anywhere

Forgive me Lord the times I forget
To give you praise that's due
I know where my help comes from
Always dear Lord, from you

Thanks for a God fearing Mom and Dad
And the bringing up that I had
Thanks for the dusting of a young man's pants
To teach me good from bad

And standing beside me all these years
Pulling me through when times were tough,
Allowing me to enjoy my children
I can never thank you enough

And thank you for the bad times Lord
I know I really should
Without bad times there's no way to know
When I really have it good

© January 2007 Clarence "Sonny" White

THE 50'S DRUG PROBLEMS

I've read it in the papers
And I've heard it on the news
About America's big drug problem
Running second, only to booze

Now I'm no country bumpkin
I've got a little smarts
Shucks, we had drug problems too
And back then it broke my heart

All week, Monday thru Friday
We were drug each day to school
To get all our book learning
So we would be nobody's fool

We were drug to Church each Sunday
On Wednesday and Sunday night
And drug out to the woodshed
If we didn't act just right

We were drug out to the cotton patch
To pick two hundred pounds a day
Then drug back to the wood shed
If that wasn't what it weighed

I remember sneaking to a movie
I knew I wasn't suppose to go
I parked my bike around in back
So mama wouldn't know

I think my sister told on me
And I cried out loud in fear
As mama drug me out the door
Holding on to my right ear

So drugs influenced our lives too
And I'm so glad it did
Too bad today's drug problems
Aren't like I had as a kid

© **January 2008 Clarence "Sonny" White**

THE FIRST CHRISTMAS

Long ago in a manger of hay
The Christ Child in that manger lay
Make music people, blow your horns
Rejoice all people, a Saviour is born

The wise men came to stay a while
And offer gifts to the Christ Child
The giving of gifts on that great day
Is why we give gifts on Christmas today

© 1951 C.H. "Sonny" White

© January 2007 Clarence "Sonny" White

***This poem was written in December 1951 by Clarence "Sonny" White at the age of 12 when in the 6th grade at Holmes School in Covington, Tennessee.

THOUGHTS OF A SNOWMAN

The snowman smiled thru teeth of coal
His carrot nose so long
Blocking from view a happy group
As they sang Christmas songs

Their joyous sounds filled the air
And made the heavens ring
The sounds were almost like
The Angels when they sang

He watched them travel door to door
As they walked across the snow
Pondering why they would sing
For folks they didn't know

He knew his time was getting short
And strained against the wind
Listening for the slightest sound
To hear those songs again

And hoping it would freeze tonight
Is the prayer that he would pray
And the sun hides its face tomorrow
So he might last another day

He knew again toward evening
The joy that it would bring
As they sang of the birth of Jesus
Our Master, Lord and King

Reflections in time

Then, he would be content to melt
And perhaps again next year
The kids would build him again
Once more those songs to hear

© October 3, 2008 Clarence "Sonny" White

WALK A MILE IN THEIR SHOES

(A tribute to our Military Men and Women)

Dad never-ever mentioned war
But we overheard in prayer
The many, many times he prayed
For the, "boys who were over there"

We knew Dad had been a Soldier
Mom said we should to be proud
But anytime Dad was home
We dare not mention it aloud

She said how brave Dad had been
He had metals in his drawer
He had been awarded
When he fought in the war

He saved a man's life before
And with bullets all around
He drug a bleeding soldier
To safer, higher, ground

He had lost very close friends
In ill-fated attacks
The ones he could depend on
The ones that watched his back

The memories too painful
He locked them in his mind
And strived to keep them hidden
Tho, they surfaced time to time

Reflections in time

So, I ask you to remember
And try to understand
As we talk to Military folks
What's going on in the man

Give them respect they deserve
Perhaps some day you'll choose
To take a stand, be the man
And walk a mile in their shoes

© January 8, 2009 Clarence "Sonny" White

WHAT I WANT FOR CHRISTMAS

Dear Lord, as we approach the day of your birth
And the year comes to an end
I give you praise and thank you Lord
The one on who I can depend

Lord, you've provided so much for me
More than words could ever say
That's why this year for Christmas
I'm asking you to take away

Take away my haughty spirit Lord
That I have from time to time
Take away any evil thoughts
I may ever have in my mind

Take away any thoughts, I did it myself
I know that simply is not true
I could never be anything myself
You allow me to excel through you

Take away any pride that I may have
I know it comes before a fall
Give me knowledge to praise you lord
And make you my all in all

Take away words you would have me not say
And anything you would not have me do
Let my mouth and my voice be a vessel God,
That's used to praise and glorify you

Reflections in time

And when my life journey is over Lord,
One last thing I would pray that you do
Take away my spirit from my body
And take it to Heaven with you

© December 10, 2003 Clarence "Sonny" White

WHAT JESUS WOULDN'T DO

A quote's been around for some time
In fact it's quite catchy too
Designed to make us stop and think
"What would Jesus do "

This quote is very well written
And although I like it too
In addition, I suggest another quote
"What Jesus wouldn't do "

Jesus wouldn't miss Church on Sunday
He wouldn't rob, kill or maim
He wouldn't talk behind his neighbors back
Or use his father's name in vain

He would never-ever seek revenge
And never refuse to forgive
Never refuse to help less fortunate folks
When he had that to give

He would never brag about himself
Never try to shift the blame
He would never do anything at all
That might bring his father shame

He would never fail to give praise to God
To whom all praise is due
He would never forget to glorify him
Like often, you and I do

The list goes on and on and on
Why folks, I'm telling you
There are so many, many things
That Jesus wouldn't do

© September 2006 Clarence "Sonny" White

WHO'S COUNTING

They were few when I was young
But surprising how they grow
And now there are so many more
Than there were years ago

Some were slow, some were fast
Then some I hardly recall
Yet some I will never forget
And those, the best of all

One when I was married
Blessed with a lovely wife
Joined by God, becoming one
To start a brand new life

One that came with children
They came with every child
How could I forget these
Looking back I always smile

Those three etched in my mind
A very proud and happy man
Assured nothing could be better
Until along came the grand

With Grandkids came even more
And I loved them every one
But who was really counting
Grandpa was having fun

With the years now adding up
And time taking its toll
The road is sometimes rocky
But, onward still I go

Now there won't be many more
But I won't be shedding tears
My Heavenly home awaits me
Lord thank you for the years

© January 2011 Clarence "Sonny" White

www.ingramcontent.com/pod-product-compliance
Ingram Content Group UK Ltd.
Pitfield, Milton Keynes, MK11 3LW, UK
UKHW041955230426
12048UKWH00008B/351